ACCRINGTON'S CHANGING FACE

by

Frank Watson & Bob Dobson

Landy Publishing
1997

First published 1997

ISBN 1 872895 31 X

British Library Cataloguing in Publication Data.
A catalogue record for this book is available from the British Library.

Landy Publishing have also published:

Accrington Observed by Brian Brindle & Bob Dobson
An Accrington Mixture edited by Bob Dobson
Concerning Clogs by Bob Dobson
In Lancashire Language: Lancashire dialect poems edited by Bob Dobson
A Lancashire Look by Benita Moore

A full list of all books published by Landy Publishing may be obtained from:
'Acorns', 3 Staining Rise, Staining, Blackpool, FY3 0BU
Tel/Fax: 01253 895678

Typeset by Mike Clarke, 41 Fountain Street, Accrington, BB5 0QR
Tel/Fax: 01254 395848

Front cover photo: A beautiful summer's day on 17th July 1907 outside Accrington Town Hall. The Mayor of Accrington had arranged a treat for the local 'crippled children' by persuading the local wealthy industrialists to donate the use of their new-fangled motor cars to take the children into the Ribble Valley, a tradition still carried on by Manchester taxi drivers who take deprived children to Blackpool.

❧ INTRODUCTION ❧

Our love of Accrington and surrounding districts Church, Oswaldtwistle, Clayton, Huncoat, Altham and Baxenden resulted in our paths crossing at Hyndburn Local History Society lectures a few years ago. We discovered that, amongst other things, we were both Accrington Grammar School old boys. Over the years we have both observed Accrington, and in our own separate ways have collected material and information about it along the way.

This book is a collection of our observations and those of many others who in times past have taken the trouble to record for posterity the Accrington of their own times. To be a local historian, all one needs to do is to record the present, because the present will become the past of the future. One day, the present will become *"the good old days"*. Fortunately, the changing face of Accrington has been pictorially recorded over the years. Someone once said, as he leaned on the railings in front of the Town Hall, *"They miss nowt round 'ere"*.

In here you'll find the work of both amateur and professional photographers. It is a distillation of the work of many former and still-present Accringtonians. If you get as much pleasure from reading the captions and looking at the photographs as we have had in compiling them, then your purchase of the book will have been worthwhile. We want to think that the book will become more precious as time goes by, and will be looked upon with affection by future generations of Accrington folk.

For the use of their photographs and their help in other ways, we want specially to thank the staff of Accrington Local History Library, John Goddard, Mike Clarke, June Huntingdon, the late Alan Breaks, Nora Davies, Roy Mawdsley and those others who have gone out of their way to help us record Accrington's Changing Face.

Bob Dobson & Frank Watson
Spring 1997

Below: The original Accrington Fish Market that stood for many years on the site of the present Fish Market. The only health and safety feature the original Fish Market had were cold water taps. Note the Lowry type male figure in the centre of the photograph with his hands behind his back, and could that be Ena Sharples behind the fish boxes to the left. The fish was displayed in very large wooden trays mounted on stone slabs supported by brick pillars. Price lists were chalked on wooden boards mounted on the rear wall behind the fish stalls.

Above: Blackburn Road with Brunswick Terrace behind prior to the Second World War when almost every street corner had its own shop. Note the rounded corner, a well-known architectural feature of a number of former buildings in Accrington.

Accrington Fire Brigade, 1940, collecting for the Civil Defence Spitfire Fund outside Will Bradshaw's, the gent's outfitters next to Woolworth's. Note the sign above the entrance door of Woolworths denoting the prices. Will Bradshaw's kitted out many generations of Grammar School boys, being the official stockist of the uniform for many years. The white markings on the car are to make it easier for pedestrians to see it in the night-time blackout conditions that were in operation at this period.

F.W.Woolworth & Co. Ltd. erected this fine building in 1924, replacing much older two-storey buildings that were formerly occupied by E.J.Riley's and McRae, watch maker and jeweller. The new 3d. and 6d. store was set a few yards further back to line up with Bridge's building on the corner so that road widening could take place. On the right of the photograph are the former underground toilets in Dutton Street. The gent's entrance is the one in the photograph, with the ladies' entrance about twenty yards further down the street. The toilets were closed down when the new toilets in Peel Street were opened with the new outside market in 1962.

J.L.Haworth's music shop, named 'Steinway House' after the famous pianos they sold, was one of the town's top stores. The new block is seen alongside a much older one, with the Slater's Arms on the far right of the picture. This was knocked down in 1936 to make room for the building of Broadway. The group photograph was taken in the newly-built Regal Cinema and Ballroom on Broadway, later to become the Odeon. Notice the artdeco style of the period. The staff from Haworth's are enjoying a splendid night of dining and dancing whilst celebrating the firm's 50th Jubilee in December 1938. *(Alan Breaks)*

J.L.Haworth's, Abbey Street, was the town's leading music shop, and was an early purveyor of televisions as well as radios and pianos. Here we see their van decorated for the 1951 Festival of Britain procession, with two employees. The firm won a prize for its decorated van in the 1953 Coronation Year procession, and we see it passing the Odeon in Broadway. The interior view of the main piano showrooms allows us to glimpse, at the rear of the Abbey Street premises, the 120 seat concert hall. *(Alan Breaks)*

J. L. Haworth & Co. —— VIEW of our MAIN PIANO SHOW ROOMS

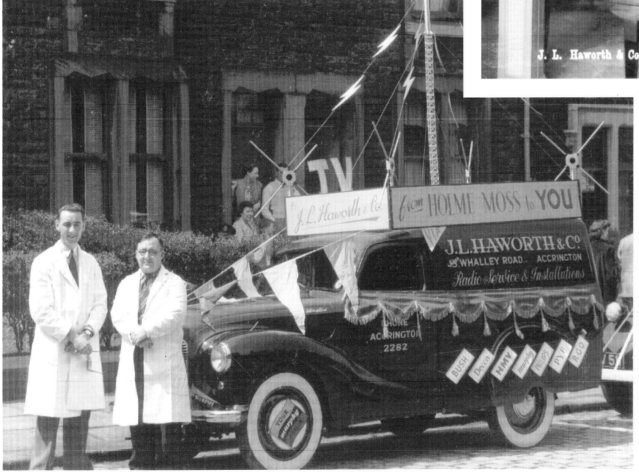

Steeplejack Joe Hurley photographed working on a local chimney. He had previously served in the army, being a member of the East Lancashire Old Comrades Association. He was involved in a fight that took place in Marquis Street in December 1934 with William Hodson, better known as Bronco Bill. Joe Hurley died from his injuries and Hodson was committed for trial three months later on a murder charge. In March 1935, Hodson was sentenced to death, but he was reprieved nine days before his execution date. *(Horace Frear)*

Pleck House formerly stood at the corner of Marquis Street and Whalley Road. When it was demolished in 1926 it was replaced by Steinway House, built for Haworth's Piano Shop. To the left of the photograph is the family maid, seated is Doctor Hannah with Mrs. Hannah standing next to him. The boy was their son, Robert Hannah (who kindly allowed me to copy this photograph in 1990), and his younger sister is sitting on the chair. Pleck Brook, a tributary of the Hyndburn, ran through the gardens of the house. Over the years he must have sold a great number of Doctor Hannah's Little Liver Pills to live in such splendour.

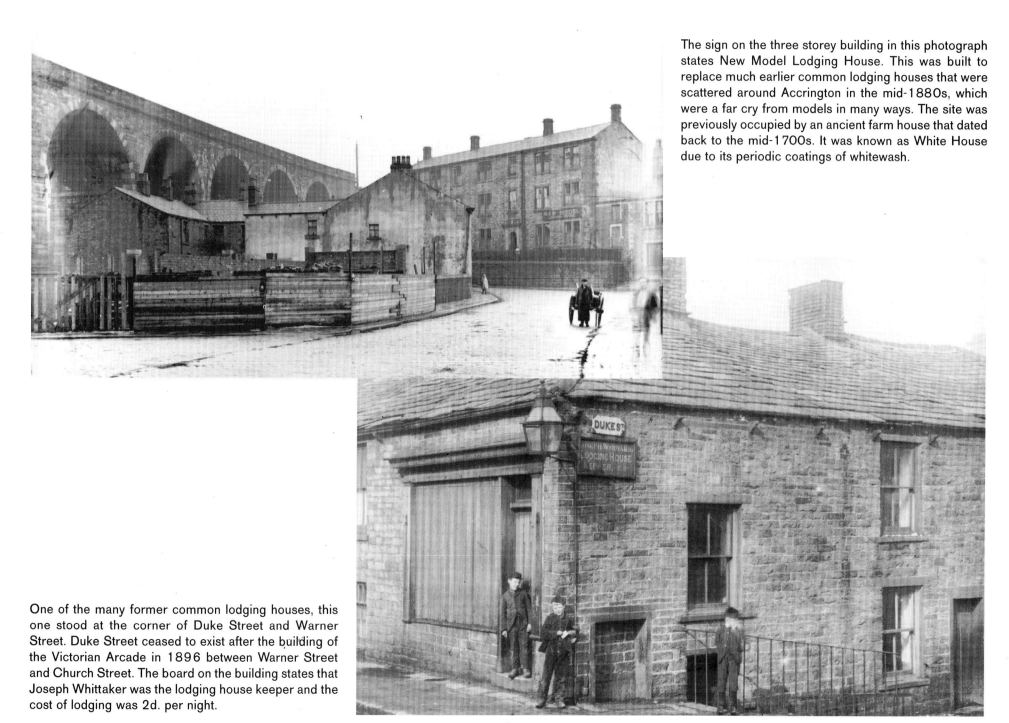

The sign on the three storey building in this photograph states New Model Lodging House. This was built to replace much earlier common lodging houses that were scattered around Accrington in the mid-1880s, which were a far cry from models in many ways. The site was previously occupied by an ancient farm house that dated back to the mid-1700s. It was known as White House due to its periodic coatings of whitewash.

One of the many former common lodging houses, this one stood at the corner of Duke Street and Warner Street. Duke Street ceased to exist after the building of the Victorian Arcade in 1896 between Warner Street and Church Street. The board on the building states that Joseph Whittaker was the lodging house keeper and the cost of lodging was 2d. per night.

Site of Accrington's outside market on Broadway after it had been removed from the Peel Street side of the Market Hall to allow the bus station to be built. The market was only located here for a few years until the new concrete outside market was opened in 1962.

Next time you hand in your library book at Accrington Library, look at the wall over your left shoulder where an enlarged copy of this photograph is mounted on the wall. It was previously part of the stage set at the Octagon Theatre, Bolton, when they performed "Accrington Pals" in 1982. The picture is of a travelling Pot Fair that used to visit Accrington every year until the early 1960s. This photograph shows the fair in about 1900, and the man standing below the gas lamp on the right-hand side has a sign around his neck which says 'Help, Blind' and in his right hand he is shaking a tin cup in which a small coin would rattle to attract attention from passers-by.

Broadway, with the formerly well-known dark-green wooden hoardings on each side of the newly-opened through-fare in 1936. Note the two mobile ice-cream carts hoping for passing trade. A good view of the back of our Town Hall, which prior to the creation of Broadway overlooked early industrial buildings, hence its lack of architectural features when compared to its splendid front and sides.

The steel-work being erected for the Regal Cinema Restaurant and Cafe, which was opened in April 1937. The cinema could seat 950 in the auditorium and 350 in the circle, with prices ranging from sixpence to one shilling and threepence. It was renamed 'The Odeon' in 1945 when it became part of a larger group of cinemas owned by Oscar Deutsch. (**ODEON** stood for Oscar Deutsch Entertains Our Nation) The cinema was built on a site formerly occupied by Myers' Stables. After many changes of name, the cinema finally closed in March 1990 to allow the site to be redeveloped.

The stone of the Market Hall still looks new - factory smoke hasn't got to it, so this photo was taken within a few years of 1869 - say 1880. It doesn't look busy enough to be a Saturday, so possibly this photo was taken on a Tuesday, the mid-week market day since 1872. The figures of Commerce, Industry and Agriculture look down on a scene so busy that the children playing and the men discussing the day's events are troubled only by a trundling wheelbarrow, and observed by a patrolling 'bobby'.

The policemen conferring in the centre of Blackburn Road may not yet be used to these new electric trams, which appeared in 1907, just before this photo was taken. The Thwaites Arms at 44 Blackburn Road has Jim Smith's name over the door, though we suspect he had departed. In the distance can be seen the finial of the Lancashire & Yorkshire Bank, corner of Eagle Street and Blackburn Road, opened in 1903. Two men can be seen carrying brew cans. Perhaps they are on the 'back' (afternoon) shift at Scaitcliffe pit. Notice Boots the Chemist on the impressive block on the left.

Here we see two photos which look along Blackburn Road in opposite directions. The Railway Hotel's licensee a century ago, Samuel Sefton, was a chap for making money. At the hotel, seen below, he had stables, arranged funerals, catered and had fingers in other businesses. Looking from his front door, he could see a policeman on point duty at the bottom of Eagle Street, spot the front door of the Nag's Head angled at the corner of School Street and Blackburn Road. On the right we can see a farmer 'kitting' milk at the bottom of Birch Street. (Is there a hidden link between Birch and School Streets? Their names may be somebody's idea of a joke.)

BLACKBURN ROAD, ACCRINGTON.

RAILWAY HOTEL,
Accrington
188

SAMUEL SEFTON,
FUNERAL ARRANGEMENTS CONDUCTED IN THE MODERN STYLE
Best Turnouts in Town for Weddings, Picnic and other Parties

Edwin Booth (smoking his pipe) took over the licence of the Park Inn, Manchester Road, from his father, who had taken it on about 1900. With Edwin here in the pub's tap room is his wife Rosina, who became licensee when Edwin died in 1952. On Edwin's left is George Cooper, *"Always the first customer to come in, every night".* *(Nora Davies)*

Originally an un-named beerhouse occupying only half of the premises seen here in 1950, the Park Inn probably took its name from the nearby Oakhill Park, opened in 1893. At the time of this photograph, the house with original railings around its front door was occupied by another family, though it is now the landlord's accomodation. The large windows close to Christ Church Street were those of the 'front room' of the pub. Notice the fire-hydrant sign on the front corner, and see that Edwin was a member of the Accrington & District Licensed Victuallers Association. *(Nora Davies)*

The aircraft posed outside Taylor Brothers' Peel Garage, next to the Broadway public house in Whalley Road, was known as the 'Flying Flea'. It was a one-man aeroplane built by John Nolan and Norman Ellison in 1935. It was taken on the back of a lorry in 1936 to Barton Aerodrome for its inaugural flight and was only used for about 3 months. Mr. Nolan is in the foreground of the picture, to the left of the propellor. Johnny Nolan was well-known as an Accrington Market Hall trader. On his stall he displayed a number of his wooden carvings.

A glossy postcard by Accrington photographer Mr. Constantine. We can see the tramlines, but no overhead power lines, so the photograph was taken after 1932, when the trams stopped running. The Palace Cinema was opened in 1915 and contained the country's first purpose-built cinema organ.

A superb photograph taken by Mr. Shaw of Blackburn captures life in Whalley Road about 1912. The King's Hall Cinema is just in view on the right edge.

This delightful picture postcard was published by Constantine's Stationers and Photographers of Accrington, but printed in Germany, making it probable that the photographer was perhaps a German too. The photograph was taken about 1908. There has been no attempt by the photographer to disguise the piles of horse muck in the roadway. Don't put your nose too close to the page!

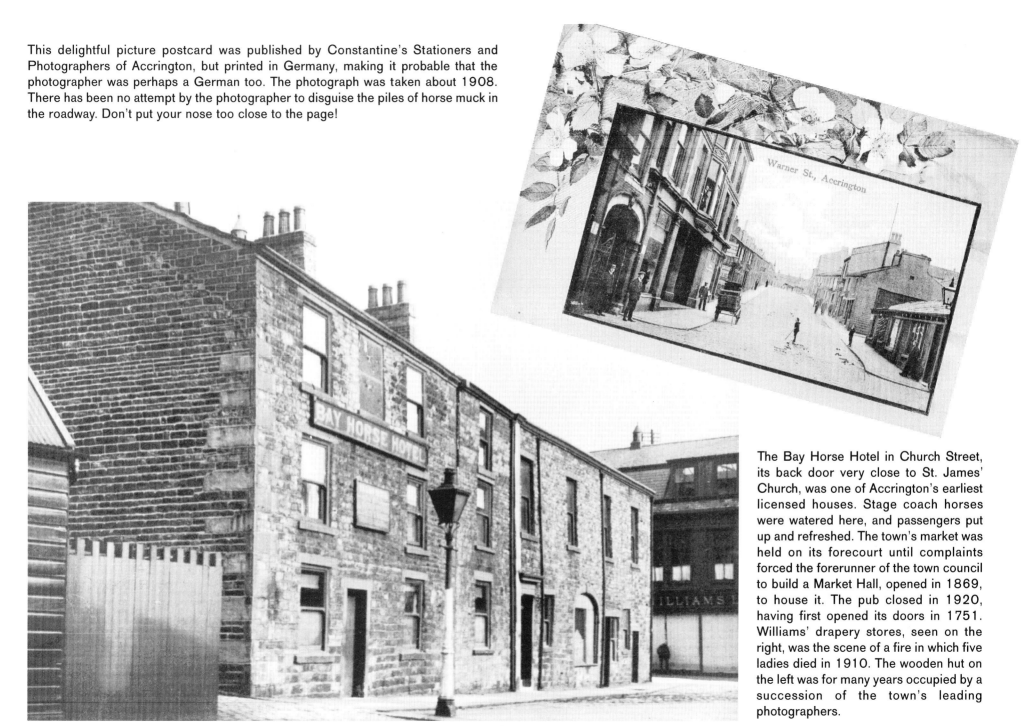

The Bay Horse Hotel in Church Street, its back door very close to St. James' Church, was one of Accrington's earliest licensed houses. Stage coach horses were watered here, and passengers put up and refreshed. The town's market was held on its forecourt until complaints forced the forerunner of the town council to build a Market Hall, opened in 1869, to house it. The pub closed in 1920, having first opened its doors in 1751. Williams' drapery stores, seen on the right, was the scene of a fire in which five ladies died in 1910. The wooden hut on the left was for many years occupied by a succession of the town's leading photographers.

An early charabanc outing, posed at the corner of Hyndburn Road, just about opposite the 'Old Black Bull', with the railings of the new St. John Ambulance building to the left.

St. John Ambulance Brigade Drill Hall photographed in 1905, one year after being officially opened by Lord Baden Powell who founded the Boy Scout movement. Note the emblem of the St. John movement just below the flag pole. The better known extension situated on King Street, that curved round the corner to join up with this building on Hyndburn Road, was erected in 1931. This extension was funded by a legacy left by a Miss A. Pilkington who resided at Laneside, on Whalley Road. Both buildings were demolished in 1985 when the area was redeveloped.

ST. JOHN AMBULANCE BRIGADE   HEADQUARTERS ACCRINGTON CORPS

DRILL HALL

HORSE AMBULANCE

The former St. Oswald's Roman Catholic Church on Hyndburn Road, opened in 1852. It ceased to be a church when Sacred Heart Roman Catholic Church, on Blackburn Road, opened in 1869. The fire that destroyed the building was spotted from a local A.R.P. post at 1.30 a.m. on 16th October, 1943. At one time, the building was being used for storing tyres. The two transepts were only slightly damaged and are now two desirable residences on Hyndburn Road.

A turn of the century view of Hyndburn Road. The gate in the foreground leads into the church yard of the Machpelah Chapel, in which was situated an old cottage which was pulled down in 1906. At this period, Hyndburn Road was known as Allom Lane. The cottage was two separate dwellings and one of them was the home of the mother of Constable Booth who had the distinction of being Accrington's first policeman. The industrial buildings in the background are now part of the ASDA car park.

The Wesleyan Methodist Chapel, commonly called simply 'Wesley' was one of the power-houses of the town, with many 'top people' attending. Its four-faced clock was the only timekeeper that many citizens had. The smaller picture shows the front door, looking onto Manchester Road at its junction with Spring Gardens. The view down Manchester Road shows Bank Terrace on the immediate right. The property on the left is part of Brook Street, demolished to make way for the Fire Station, Courts and Police Station in the mid-1930s. Wesley's tower is undergoing repairs. Notice also the chapel's schoolrooms, where Sunday School and many other chapel activities were held.

Three views of Abbey Street, one of the town's main thoroughfares since the days of the turnpikes. It was constructed in 1790/91 as part of the Whalley to Bury turnpike.

Left and below: The same spot seen from different angles, with Oak Street opposite Plantation Street. The ornate lamp standards have been replaced by more functional, planer ones in a motorised, electrical age.

Bottom left: The town's first Post Office, here since at least 1818, captured by Thomas Walton, professional photographer for fifty years with a studio in Abbey Street from the turn of the century. Tasker Street is just out of view to the right.

Early in the century we look up Whalley Road from the railway viaduct and see Owen Street on the right, opposite Milnshaw Lane and Knowlmere Street on the left. The absence of motor cars on this main road is the reason why the Clock Garage has not yet been built on the site of Owen Farm.

Whalley Road Methodist Church was close-by others of that denomination in Union Street, Abbey Street and Cambridge Street, and when this photograph was taken in the late 1920s, all would be full each Sunday. Running alongside the church was Kenyon Street, also called 't'Pleck'. We get a glimpse of the corner door of the Castle Hotel and a good look at the standard carrying power for the trams.

22

St. John's Parish Church was in a healthy financial position when it could afford to build for its vicar a splendid vicarage on Burnley Road, and the vicar was in a position to afford to employ maids who we see peeping out of the side door in Arago Street.

191 AVENUE PARADE AND COPPICE, ACCRINGTON.

We can see what a fine street of substantial houses built of local stone Avenue Parade is when it isn't cluttered up with motor cars. Possibly this shot captures a moment when a local farmer was delivering milk kept in kits on his horse-drawn float, to be delivered to housewives in their jugs. The absence of people suggests that the photograph was taken very early on a Sunday morning.

King Street, looking towards "The Blockade" public house, with the Prince's Theatre the tall building in the background. The only structures still standing from this 1950s photograph are "The Blockade" and the railway viaduct. The second shop, behind the van, was Musgrove's, a well-known chemist's shop for many years.

This photograph, dated about 1900, was taken from roughly the same spot as the one above but looking in the other direction, towards Milnshaw Lane. This area around Bull Bridge was the original centre of Old Accrington. The only remaining part of this photograph is the stone parapet, on the right-hand side of the bridge over the River Hyndburn, on which is carved "C. C. Lower Bridge Accrington". Accrington Higher Bridge was situated near the Bridge Inn in Church Street.

Old cottages, next to Bugle Yard just off Grange Lane, being demolished in the 1930s. They are now the site of the police garage. The building behind the cottages was the Iron, Tin & Copper Plate Works of Henry Slack. Look for the cowl on the roof and compare the photograph with the engraving.

In the centre of the photograph is the Toll-house, built in 1796 at a cost of eighty pounds for the Bury to Whalley Turnpike Trust. It stood at the junction of Grange Lane and Manchester Road.

25

As part of the local salvage drive during the Second World War, the cannon that overlooked Accrington from the top of the Coppice are being loaded onto a local council wagon, supervised by Mr. Fishwick on the right.

Making munitions at Howard & Bulloughs during the Second World War, part of the local war effort. At this period, this one firm employed some five thousand people. Many local firms were switched to essential war work, using mainly female workers. *(Frances Wilkinson)*

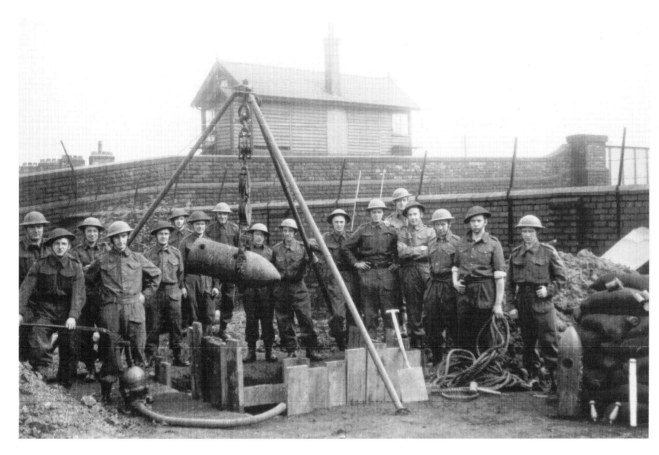

The signalman in Church East signal box, which overlooked Lonsdale Street in Accrington, had a bird's-eye view of the local Home Guard on a training exercise, in the early 1940s, on how to deal with U.X.B.s or unexploded bombs.

The two photographs on the right show what extensive damage bombs can cause when they do explode on impact. The remains of a house in Clayton-le-Moors that was struck by a bomb and a crater nearby. The bombs fell on the night of 19th/20th June 1940.

Brickworks needed brick-built chimneys, and both these views show off both bricks and chimneys, monuments to the bricklayer's craft. Below we glimpse the Baxenden brickworks, linked to the railway. The site was operated by the Lancashire Brick & Terra Cotta Company (Baxenden) Ltd. between 1893 and 1904. It had its own quarry on the site. Above, the view of the Accrington Brick & Tile Company's works, where NORI bricks were made for the world, is seen looking down Whinney Hill, with the Greyhound pub around the corner to the right. The group photograph is of workmen at the NORI works around the turn of the century. Thomas Quinn, seen on the left at the end of the second row wearing his cap back-to-front, had worked there since he was ten years old, walking from Clayton each day. *(Tony Kershaw)*

A typical preparation room in a local weaving shed at the turn of the century, where twisting and drawing of the warp is taking place. The location is not known.

A very rare postcard view of Cocker Lumb Mill, Oswaldtwistle, taken in the late 1800s. This mill, first recorded in 1810 but possibly dating from the 18th century, was originally worked by James Grimshaw of Ramsclough. The mill closed as long ago as 1911, and piecemeal demolition followed. There is now hardly any trace of this old mill.

Left: Coal tubs that have just been wound up the shaft at Scaitcliffe Colliery. Note the low height of the tubs due to the narrow seams that were worked at this pit.

Bottom left: The coal weigh-bridge at Broad Oak Pit, which closed in 1939.

Below: The all-wooden winding gear supports at Scaitcliffe Colliery which were unusual as most were constructed of metal. Note the pile of pit props in the foreground which do not appear to be very long, another indication of the low coal seams which forced the colliery to close in 1962.

Two coalminers in a posed photograph taken at Broad Oak Pit. The one on the right is Mr. Maden who worked in other local pits after Broad Oak closed. *(B. Maden)*

A wooden printing block that was used to place the trade mark on cloth printed at Broad Oak. On the death of Robert Hargreaves, in 1854, the firm was leased to F.W.Grafton who purchased it in 1880. As the trade mark shows, hand block printing was superceded by printing from engraved rollers.

Note all the preparations that had taken place at Broad Oak Works for the visit, in 1913, by King George and Queen Mary during their tour of East Lancashire.

Broad Oak's own fire engine and staff, plus horse in the shafts, ready to set off to a fire-brigade exhibition held in Accrington in the early 1900s. At this period, many local firms had fire appliances manned and operated by their own staff.

Broad Oak, Reading Room.

Accrington.

J. A. Hanson, Accrington.

Broad Oak Reading Room which was situated by the side of the main entrance to the works, just off Manchester Road. It was built for the employees of Broad Oak in an effort to provide various types of recreational facilities. Just behind the building was a crown bowling green. These facilities were enjoyed by many generations of Broad Oak employees.

As well as 'NORI' and 'STANLEY', the word 'EWBANK' was synonymous with 'ACCRINGTON'. Household products, predominantly the carpet sweeper bearing this name, had been made by Entwisle and Kenyon here since the 1860s. We see the mangle shop in full production during the 1920s. The wooden rolers had been turned in the Hyndburn Road works, and probably the iron frames had been cast here too. The company were into advertising on a big scale and attended the 1924 British Empire Exhibition at Wembley, which is where we see their stand. All the employees were taken on trains overnight to see the great international event. The works was bought out by the Prestige Group and closed down in 1983. The site is now occupied by the ASDA Store.

33

This splendid photograph was taken inside Whittaker's foundry in Dowry Street about 1910. Started in 1854 by Christopher Whittaker and his brother Thomas, the company became 'C. Whittaker & Co.' in 1900, producing brick-making and similar machinery for the world. Their telegraphic address was 'Bricks, Accrington'. (Gordon Parker)

Here we see the inside of Broadley's print works, Clayton, about 1936, with a proliferation of pulleys providing the power for the machines. The style of the workmen's overalls is known as "bib and brace". *(Mrs. Carol Baker)*

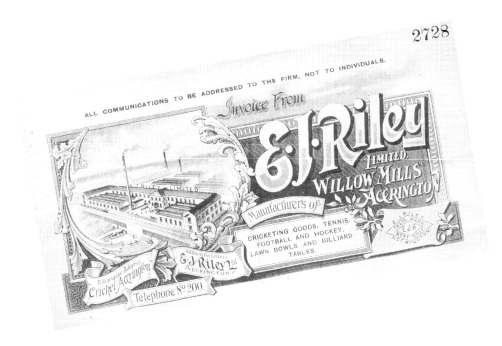

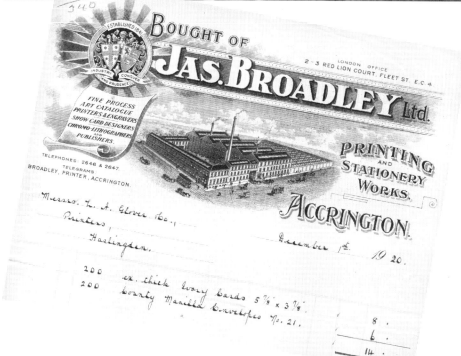

The name of E.J.Riley's, sports outfitters, was synonymous with Accrington wherever snooker and billiards were played. They made their own cricket bats and everything connected with a multitude of sports at their premises in Dale Street and Willow Street. The Company is now based in Padiham.

The original boiler house at Stonebridge Mill in Oswaldtwistle, built in 1845-46, with an early type of Lancashire boiler. Note the size of the shovel that the fire-beater is leaning on. Is it any wonder he appears to need a rest?

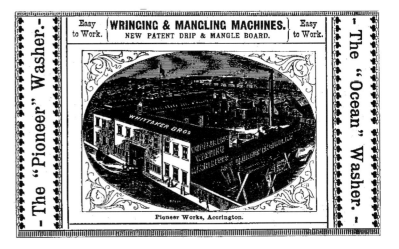

Some very young mill operatives posing for the camera in the early 1900s at Hoyle Bottom Mill in Oswaldtwistle. The site is now a lovely garden and the arches that once housed the tacklers' benches now shelter many varieties of flowers. Many of the original stone flags of this weaving shed are still in situ in the garden. Hoyle Bottom Mill went into liquidation in 1931, and most of the buildings were demolished shortly afterwards.

The administrative offices of Accrington Corporation Electricity Works on Hyndburn Road. They were built in 1899-1900 and are one of the few buildings of this era that are still standing in 1996. Note the gasometer in the background.

This photograph reveals the true size of the Moorfield Colliery and Coke Works which were located by the side of the canal in Altham. This complex had a railway connection, via Nori Brick Works, to a small siding by the side of Accrington Cricket Club. In 1883, this colliery was rocked by an explosion that left 64 men and boys dead. Their names are recorded on a memorial tablet in Altham Church.

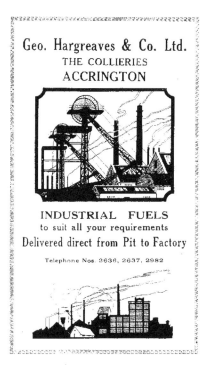

The earliest known photograph taken of a fair on Ellison's Tenement. The annual Accrington Fair had to move to this site in 1886 with the opening of the steam tramways. Prior to this date, the fairs were located in Peel Street. Note the gasometer in the top left corner which was on Hyndburn Road.

Arrival of the annual fair in Accrington just after the turn of the century. The fair wagons did not make their way direct to Ellison's Tenement but toured the main roads of the town first for publicity purposes. The stage coach with a team of eight horses has just passed under the railway bridge on Whalley Road, Accrington.

The original 'Hippodrome' building which opened on 12th October 1903, with admission charges which ranged from 2d. to a shilling. Miss Ella and her Forest Bred Lions topped the bill on the opening night. This building burnt down on 26th June 1908, to be immediately replaced by a more permanent red-brick structure. This 'New Hippodrome' opened on 21st Decemeber 1908, a mere six months later. It is hard to credit that such a substantial building, with a seating of 1800, could be erected in such a short space of time.

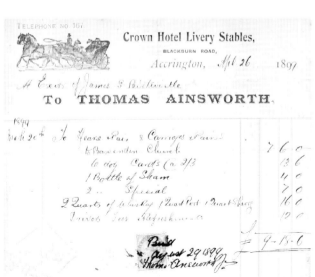

The smouldering ruins of the original 'Hippodrome' on the morning of 27th June 1908.

A very rare postcard of Accrington Engine Shed shortly after it was opened in 1899 at a cost of £51,859. The Northern Light type of roof was replaced in 1936. Notice the large wooden doors on each road into the shed. The last steam engine to leave this depot was transferred to Rose Grove in March 1961. From this date only Diesel Multiple Units were maintained until the shed closed in 1972. The site, after a short period of use as a fairground, has now been developed for housing.

LY.R. Engine Shed Acc.

ACCRINGTON RAILWAY SMASH. July 17/1913   (Walton's)

This crash occurred at 2.10 a.m. on the 17th July 1913 when the 10.20 p.m. goods train from Rochdale to Fleetwood ran away down Accrington Bank and became derailed on leaving the sand drag, near Accrington South Signalbox, through which the signalman had diverted the train. It then crashed into the 11.00 p.m. goods train from Preston to Moston which was standing on the 'Up Fork Line', waiting for a clear road. At the time the crash took place there were no footplate staff on the runaway train. (But that's another story) The official report into the crash makes very interesting reading.

Remodelling of the Nuttall Street Bridge taking place in 1936. The original bridge was constructed in 1846, but the restricted height of the opening caused problems for many years. On the right are before and after photographs taken from roughly the same spot.

When the bridge was being constructed in 1846, it was reputed that a young girl was murdered and her body hidden behind the partially completed stonework of the bridge. The stone masons carved the girl's initials on a stone with a small matchstick figure next to the initials. This original stone was incorporated into the bridge when it was remodelled in 1936. (Guess which stone was lost when the bridge was recently demolished) This story has been handed down through generations of families living in the Woodnook area.

Lonsdale Street was certainly busy when this photographer captured a horse drawing a water cart on the wrong side of the road as it hurried down towards Blackburn Road.

Very few photographs exist of Baxenden Railway Station, built in the 1840s by the East Lancashire Railway, which later became the Lancashire & Yorkshire Railway. Amalgamation in 1923 created the London Midland and Scottish Railway, and the notice boards retain this name even in this post-nationalisation view. Taken in the 1960s, it looks uphill towards Haslingden.

Seen here about 1930, Accrington Station's large forecourt was packed with holidaymakers each Bank Holiday and every day during the July holiday week.

Christ Church (C of E) had its own school, and here we see one of the classes - 'Standard' was the name given to a particular year - in the last decade of the century. Young Edwin Booth, who became licensee of the Park Inn, is one of the twenty scholars. In 1997, the school building has been adapted for housing. *(Nora Davies)*

New Jerusalem (Swedenborgian) Church was a major influence on the development of Accrington. The church's school premises were on Hargreaves Street, exactly where the present church stands, on the right looking down Adelaide Street. The man standing in the doorway in this end-of-century view is probably Jeremiah Brigg, a long-serving caretaker.

The three photos here are of Clayton at different periods, as illustrated by the variety of the transport. The Hare & Hounds pub, with the Load of Mischief pub opposite, is seen just a few years before 1907, when the steam trams were replaced with electric ones, needing overhead power. Beneath it is a 1920s view of the road near what is now the link road to the motorway. The above photo shows a party out in waggonettes calling for some Nuttall's Ale at the Petre Arms, Blackburn Road, Clayton. The building is still there, it is Holt Mill House, close by Holt Mill Bridge, the dip in the road at the boundary of Clayton and Rishton. The pub's licence was transferred to the Dunkenhalgh Hotel.

Grange Street, Clayton, captured a few years before the First World War. The lads hoop was probably made of iron. All were most interested in the photographer taking their photograph. The road surface looks unmade, as does the pavement, with a few flagstones outside two garden gateposts.

A photograph probably taken by Claytonian Mary Chatburn about 1910, when Asquith was P.M., and Women's Suffrage was on the political agenda. A jazz band and some characters, one of them possibly a bogus policeman, make this a very special photograph.

The man reading his newspaper is sat on the wall of the Lamb Inn, Whalley Road, Clayton. The photograph was probably taken about 1915 when the shop below the 'X', No.319, was kept by grocer Mark Jepson.

Clayton-le-Moors Brass Band: location unknown. On the large drum are the words 'Prize Band' which seems to have been painted on much later than the lettering above. The photograph could have been taken to celebrate them winning the 5th prize of £2 at a brass band contest held at Stalybridge on 21st August 1875. Out of 36 bands entered for the competition, 28 turned up, so coming fifth was a good result, hence the addition of 'Prize Band' on the drum.

Enfield Mill was the first large mill erected in Clayton, by Robert Clagg in 1834-35. The factory ceased production in 1933 and the only remaining building today is Millfield House on the left which was formerly the Mill Master's residence.

The Whitsuntide chapel processions were a major event in Huncoat's year. Here, left, we see part of one which took place about 1912, with village dignitaries leading the way, and on the 1907 photograph, right, we see another group of behatted village elders in a relaxed mood.

TELEPHONE Nº 132.

Manufacturers of
SANITARY PIPES.
FIRE BRICKS.
TILES.
SANITARY WARE.
&c. &c.

Bought of

TELEGRAMS.
STEPHENSON, HUNCOAT, ACCRINGTON.

Manufacturers of
IMPROVED PATENT
WASTE WATER CLOSETS
AND LATRINES FOR
DWELLING HOUSES &
PUBLIC BUILDINGS.

HENRY STEPHENSON & SON,
HUNCOAT, ACCRINGTON.

This bill-heading was sent by Henry Stephenson to Mr. Schofield Birtwistle in 1899. Notice that the firm had their own railway sidings, linked to the Accrington to Burnley line, seen in the background.

The corner at Church Commercial when one could walk into the middle of the road to board a tram without the worries about other traffic. The fourth male from the left has a certain sartorial elegance not usually associated with the male population of Church at this period. Perhaps he has been trying to impress the two young ladies stood behind him who seem more interested in the older gentleman about to board the tram.

In the bottom lefthand corner is a marching military band followed by horse-drawn artillery, with foot soldiers bringing up the rear. This photograph, taken prior to 1886 (there are no tramlines) could be part of an army recruiting campaign. The tall building behind the telegraph pole is the canal warehouse at Church.

One of the many processions held to celebrate the Coronation of King George Fifth and Queen Mary in 1911. This one is passing along Union Road, Oswaldtwistle, and the horse-drawn float has just passed Saint Paul's School. Wearing of hats for both sexes would appear to be compulsory looking at this photograph.

One of the many former inns and beerhouses on Market Street, Church, at the turn of the century. This is the relatively unknown 'Musicians Inn' at 61 Market Street, Church, which stood on the corner of Gordon Street just below the railway bridge. It lost its licence prior to 1909 and then became a private house for many years. In the late 1970s it became the site of a small local police station which only lasted about ten years.

Looking towards Blackburn from Church Commercial, the shop on the corner of Market Street, opposite the canal company's warehouse, sells Cope's Mixture, a patent medicine to ease the coughing of mill workers choked with cotton and coal fumes. The canal warehouse was originally built for the Hargreaves of Broad Oak Print Works. Perhaps this photograph was taken early on Sunday morning, as it has only one person on it.

Paddock House was built by Benjamin Walmsley in 1830. The Walmsley family originated from Rough Hey and were responsible for the building of Moscow Mill. Paddock House is best remembered as part of the buildings of Paddock House Convent School.

172 PADDOCK HOUSE, OSWALDTWISTLE.

On the last Friday night in October 1927, a gale caused havoc throughout Lancashire. Here we see the remains of the chimney of the Providence Mill at Tanpits, owned by the Antley Manufacturing Company. It had been 120 feet high, and fell without damaging any of the surrounding buildings, leaving about 50 feet standing. Crowds came to see the collapsed chimney, built of hand-made bricks, and to watch the repairs being effected to it over the weekend to allow the firm's 650 looms to continue in operation on Monday morning.

CROSS AND RHYDDINGS ST OSWALDTWISTLE

View down Rhyddings Street from Rhyddings Park in the days when the local mill chimneys were still smoking. The cross in the foreground, a memorial to the old Oswaldtwistle Market Cross, was donated by William Walmsley Simpson and his wife in the coronation year of 1911.

Laying the cobbled setts in Union Road, Oswaldtwistle, precise date of the photograph unknown. To the right of the temporary barriers is the 'Star Inn' which was demolished at the turn of the century to be replaced by new property in 1904, which is now used as a dental surgery by Garnetts. Note the large kerbstones on the left of the photograph.

These two photographs reflect the importance to Edwardians of the church procession. In the 1911 Coronation procession, seen here at the top end of Union Road, people were keen to be associated with the banner of their church or chapel. In the St. Paul's photograph we can contrast the fine walking dresses of the girls with the everyday smock dresses, noting that all the lads are wearing caps, and that several ladies are wearing shawls over their heads. The building on the right was Oswaldtwistle Town Hall, now the Hyndburn Civic Theatre.

52

This brickwork's 1940s meal-time game is interesting if only because the left-handed batter is the legendary Eddie Paynter of Enfield, Lancashire and England, whose name will forever be recorded in every book written about the Ashes for his lion-hearted performances against the Aussies in Brisbane in 1932/33.

The 1905 Derby match, Church-v-Accrington, has drawn a good crowd to the West End ground. Note the wooden Aspen railway viaduct in the background.

Perhaps the policeman is present at this June 1905 match at Enfield because it was a police charity match. The original photograph on a postcard suggests that he may have been called Jack and was stationed at Altham. Why wasn't he paying attention to the lads getting a free look-in over the cricket club wall?

The horse-drawn laundry van belonged to the Co-op Laundries, one of several in the Accrington area. The company was formed by several Societies co-operating with each other to provide laundry services to East Lancashire housewives and businesses. The enterprise closed down in the early 1960s.

The canal at Church was a busy thoroughfare up to the 1950s when the transportation of goods and fuel transferred to the roads. This photograph was taken about 1920 and shows a steam barge towing two dumb barges. The barge tied up closest to the camera is loaded with acid carboys.

On 7th May 1935, a procession passes the Black Dog pub in Union Road, Ossie. The leading lorry is owned and driven by Allan Stock, owner of a mineral water firm based in Burnley Road. The procession celebrated the Silver Jubille of King George and Queen Mary.
(Alan Breaks)

It was a proud day for Accrington when the town acquired a cottage (i.e. small) hospital in 1897 through the generosity of local employers and workers and the members of the Independent Order of Oddfellows, a society promoting welfare for its members and others. Here we see the now-enlarged hospital and inside the Children's Ward about 1920. The original 'cottage' part is to the left of the chimney.

VICTORIA HOSPITAL, ACCRINGTON.

MANCHESTER UNITY, I. O. ODDFELLOWS.

THE

Foundation Stone

OF THE

COTTAGE HOSPITAL

WILL BE LAID BY

HIS WORSHIP THE MAYOR,

Alderman Haywood, J.P.,

On Saturday, October 26th, 1895.

Members of the several Lodges in the Accrington District are cordially invited to take part in the Demonstration, and meet the District and Lodge Officers, at the Commercial Hotel, and Bridge Inn, Church Street.

Further particulars will be announced in the local papers.

Every Member is urged to be present, and assist in making the inauguration of so worthy an Institution a success.

JOHN E. ELLIS, Prov. G.M.
A. E. BRITCLIFFE, D. Prov. G.M.
JOHN E. GILL, Prov. C.S.

Two early forms of transport used by the wealthy families in the district. On the right are the imposing gates to Broad Oak House, Accrington, during the period when it was owned by the Macalpine family. Mr. Macalpine is being driven by his coachman, Mr. Kay, down the snow covered drive enroute to one of his many businesses in the area.

One of the first motorcars in the district was owned by the Lomax Family of Clayton Hall. It is photographed outside their stables where they kept their otter-hunting dogs. The top half of the door is covered by feet cut off captured otters.

Transport used by the working class. On the left is a mothers' outing that follows the fashionable trend of the period that everyone should wear a hat; even the driver conforms. How far this group travelled is unknown, but they set off from Plantation Street, Accrington.

This early local bus service is photographed outside the barn that was originally next to the Hyndburn Bridge public house. Lobers ran a bus service between Great Harwood, Clayton and Altham. The service ceased after a serious accident on the 19th February 1915. Lobers' bus left the Hare and Hounds, Clayton, at 6.50 a.m. enroute to Calder Pit, Altham, with over forty miners on board. Due to the failure of the steering gear, the bus hit a kerb on the bend near Moorside Farm then crashed into a stone wall before overturning, injuring many of the passengers. The driver was a Mr. John William of Tremellen Street, Accrington.

An entry for a local carnival procession stood outside the Ragged School in Jacob Street, Accrington. The horse looks far from ragged with its harness all decorated. J.&T.Livesey's had their premises in Livesey Street, and were advertising their plumbing and heating business on a lovely sunny carnival day.

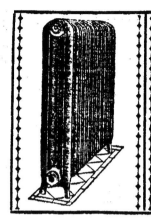

ACCRINGTON MARKET SHOPPING WEEK,

Friday, September 2nd, to Saturday, September 10th, 1910.
Both Days Inclusive.

LIST OF CHEAP FARES AND TIMES
OF DEPARTURE AND RETURN BY
LANCASHIRE AND YORKSHIRE RAILWAY.
On dates as shown below.

FROM:	Tuesday, Sep. 6, & Sats., Sept. 3 & 10. Return Fares 3rd Class	Times	Saturdays, September 3rd and 10th Times	Return Fares 3rd Class
BACUP	1/3	Any Train after one o'clock	12 39 1 20	1/3
STACKSTEADS			12 34 1 24	1/2
WATERFOOT			12 37 1 27	1/1
CLOUGHFOLD	1/1½		12 40 1 30	1/0
RAWTENSTALL			12 43 1 33	1/0
EWOOD BRIDGE	1/1		1 37	1/1
STUBBINS			1 42	1/1
RAMSBOTTOM			1 4 1 56	1/1
HELMSHORE	8½d.		1 11 2 3	8½d.
HASLINGDEN	4½d.		1 18 2 9	4½d.
BAXENDEN	3d.		1 20* 2 13	3d.
COLNE	No Bookings on Tuesdays		1 8 1 44	1/3
NELSON			1 15 1 52	1/0
BRIERFIELD			1 20 1 56	1/0
BURNLEY (MCHR. ROAD)	9d.	12 50*		
BURNLEY (BANK TOP)	9d.	1 3*		
BURNLEY BARRACKS	9d.	1 6*		
ROSE GROVE	7d.	1 10*		
HAPTON	4½d.	1 14*		
HUNCOAT	3d.	1 18*		
BLACKBURN	7d.	1 8*		
RISHTON	4d.	1 16*		
CHURCH	2d.	1 20*		
GT. HARWOOD	1/0	2 54*		
SIMONSTONE	10½d.	2 19*	1 28*	
PADIHAM	9d.	2 22*	1 31*	

* These are the first available trains, but you can proceed by any ordinary train after these times.

PASSENGERS RETURN by any train after 5.55 p.m. for all parts.

For any further details see Lancashire and Yorkshire Time Books, or enquire at any railway station.

A new addition to Accrington Corporation's bus fleet. Many of Accrington's early buses were single deckers due to the many low bridges in the locality.

Accrington Corporation bus number 78 in traditional livery of dark blue with red and gold lining plus gilt ornate lettering and Coat of Arms. Note the unusual guard rails on the side of the bus between the front and rear axles. The two man crew are awaiting departure time.

This machine, known as a 'Celerity', was purchased by Accrington Corporation Tramways Department in 1918 so that the maintenance of trackwork could be done by direct labour instead of outside contractors. It was a horse-drawn portable rail-grinding machine and cost £76-17s-3d. It saved the expense of having to remove the cobbles and then replace damaged rails. With power taken from the overhead catenary, damaged rails could be repaired on site at greatly reduced expense. The machine with its three operatives is in the Dyke Nook area of Whalley Road, Accrington.

The fastest milkman in the West End at the entrance lodge gates to the driveway that led up to Paddock House when it was a private residence. Note the iron railings to stop people from the houses on Frederick Street encroaching onto the private driveway.

One of Accrington's many local characters of the 1920s, Michael James MacNamara was born in 1891 and lived most of his life at 12 Robert Nuttall Street, which is now known as Belfield Road. Despite being a cripple, he carried on a business as a firelighter hawker and was well-known in Woodnook and Higher Antley districts. He must have fallen on hard times in later life as he died in Pike Lowe Workhouse which later became part of Rossendale General Hospital.

At the top of King Street, corner of Albion Street, this shop is No.126 Blackburn Road. It appears here to be a well-stocked grocery shop around the time of the First World War. In the 1950s it was in use as a grocery and pie shop, with a small cafe area in the back where pie and peas were served by Mr. & Mrs. Wells for under two shillings. By the mid-1990s it had ceased to be a shop, although the original leaded windows were still intact.

Crown Hotel Livery Stables,
BLACKBURN ROAD,
Accrington, Nov 29 188

To ROBERT ROSKELL, Jr.,

POSTING IN ALL ITS BRANCHES

CAB PROPRIETOR, &c.

"*Little Jack*" Silver, a diminutive Jewish man, kept a shop on Blackburn Road, firstly under the railway arches, then later, in the 1950s, by Kendall's Temperance Hotel, corner of Fox Street. Under war-time conditions, he sold anything he could obtain, later specialising in clothing. 13 years-old Bob Dobson bought his first pair of long pants from "*Little Jack's*"

Established 1875.

KING STREET,

Telephones—0275. 0275A.

Accrington, May 15 1909

Mrs Sarsfield

Dr. to JOHN WILSON,

IRONMONGER & WHITESMITH.

Miss DOROTHY SLATER

Accrington
Armless
Wonder
Girl

In the early 1930s, Dorothy Slater's family, who lived in Pendle Street, raised money for their daughter, born without arms in the mid-20s, by producing and selling postcards. Here we see the front and back of one of them. It appears that Dorothy has signed her name, as shown in the picture, after someone else had written the brief message. Dorothy was the last of five children, and her mother was quite old when Dorothy was born, which possibly explains Dorothy's deformity. It is known that she could pick up pennies with her toes and held a cup of tea this way. At one time she worked on a fairground. She died in the 1960s.

About 1960, a young lad walked around Accrington on a Sunday morning with a camera and captured this lady at the front door of her house in Oak Street. She was typical of thousands of Lancashire housewives in her pinny, clogs and headscarf, her sleeves rolled up for work. Notice the stairs immediately behind the front door. The window above the arch is probably one of the bedrooms in her house. *(Alan Fitton)*

Accrington's first motor ambulance in the yard of the tramway depot, with the red-brick wall of the Hippodrome beyond the wooden gates. The driver is a Mr. Harry Williams who was on call 24 hours every day. The motor ambulance was donated to Accrington by Miss Haworth of Hollins Hill in memory of her brother Mr. William Haworth who died on 25th September 1915. Note the Accrington Coat of Arms between the two windows.

Joseph Briggs, at 17 years of age, left Accrington for a life in America, where he became the manager of the famous Tiffany Studio, designers and manufacturers of fine artistic glass products. In 1932, after the company's closure, he shipped some of the beautiful Tiffany glass vases and lamps to Accrington, giving around 140 pieces to the Corporation. Those exquisite vases and lamps now form a collection rated as the best in Europe and are housed in the Haworth Art Gallery (another gift to the town). Here is a rare photograph of Joseph and his wife Elizabeth. *(The Briggs Family)*

They didn't need alarm clocks in the old days. A couple of short taps from the long pole of the knocker-up would soon inform Oswaldtwistle folk it was time to get up. This photograph is of Mr. Hiram Taylor walking down Worsley Street where he lived. He was known locally as the "Human alarm clock" and he finally retired in 1960 at the age of eighty-two. To save breaking the glass in bedroom windows, knockers-up always fastened fine metal wires to the end of their poles. A wonderful thing is education.

This fine old gentleman was born in Scotland in 1771 and died in Haslingden in 1882 at the ripe old age of one hundred and one. His real name was John McKenzie and in his youth he was in the Scots Greys and fought at the Battle of Waterloo in 1815. In the Haslingden and Accrington area he was better known as 'Long-Me-Dong' because of a refrain he sang when walking along the local streets selling the sulphur matches he made. He advertised his wares by calling out "Long and Strong" in his thick Scottish accent, hence his nickname. His grave is in the churchyard of Haslingden Parish Church.